A Killer Whale's World

written and illustrated by Caroline Arnold

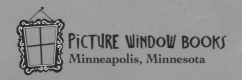

PICTURE WINDOW BOOKS
Minneapolis, Minnesota

Special thanks to our advisers for their expertise:

Marcy Kober, Education Curator
The Whale Museum
Friday Harbor, Washington

Susan Kesselring, M.A., Literacy Educator
Rosemount–Apple Valley–Eagan
(Minnesota) School District

Editor: Christianne Jones
Designer: Nathan Gassman
Page Production: James Mackey
Creative Director: Keith Griffin
Editorial Director: Carol Jones
The illustrations in this book were created with cut paper.

Picture Window Books
5115 Excelsior Boulevard
Suite 232
Minneapolis, MN 55416
877-845-8392
www.picturewindowbooks.com

Printed in the United States of America.

Library of Congress Cataloging-in-Publication Data
Arnold, Caroline.
A killer whale's world / written and illustrated by Caroline Arnold.
p. cm. – (Caroline Arnold's black & white animals)
Includes bibliographical references and index.
ISBN 1-4048-1321-7 (hard cover)
1. Killer whale–Juvenile literature. I. Title.

QL737.C432A762 2005
599.53'6–dc22   2005023163

This book is about killer whales.
They are also called orcas.

Where killer whales live: in oceans all over the world
Habitat: ocean
Food: fish and sea animals
Length of males: 25 to 30 feet (7.6 to 9.1 meters)
Length of females: 22 to 25 feet (6.7 to 7.6 m)
Weight of males: 8,000 to 12,000 pounds (3,600 to 5,400 kilograms)
Weight of females: 3,000 to 8,000 pounds (1,350 to 3,600 kg)
Animal class: mammals
Scientific name: *Orca orcinus*

A killer whale baby is called a calf. Dive into the ocean and journey along with a killer whale calf and learn about a killer whale's world.

Out in the ocean, a family of killer whales swims toward shore. Their smooth bodies slide through the cool, salty water. Waves splash against the tall fins on the whales' backs.

Whales live in family groups called pods. A killer whale pod usually has between five and 50 whales in it.

The group stops when they reach a quiet spot.
One of the whales is ready to have a baby.

The baby killer whale is born underwater. He looks small next to his mother, but he is nearly 8 feet (2.4 m) long and weighs more than 400 pounds (180 kg). He is already as big as a large refrigerator!

A spout is formed by water droplets in the whale's warm breath. It is like the tiny cloud your breath makes when you are outside on a cold day.

The mother whale pushes her new baby up to the surface. He takes his first breath. Air goes in through the blowhole on the top of his head and moves to the lungs. When he breathes out, he makes a misty spout.

The baby killer whale is hungry. He slips underwater and nuzzles his mother's belly. He drinks some of her rich milk. After a few seconds he comes up to the surface to breathe again.

Blubber is a thick layer of fat that grows under a whale's skin. It helps keep the whale warm.

Day by day, the baby killer whale's body becomes bigger and rounder. Day by day, the baby grows stronger.

The baby whale can swim as soon as he is born.
But he cannot swim as fast as the other whales.
He stays beside his mother.

As the pod cruises the ocean, the mother and baby whales stay at the center. The adult males swim on the outside of the pod.

Her powerful tail pushes her through the water. The wave next to her body pulls the baby along with her. The mother and the baby can keep up with the other whales this way.

Killer whales have big appetites. An adult killer whale can eat up to 300 pounds (135 kg) of food a day.

The baby whale follows his mother as the pod searches for food. "Click, click, click," they call. The echoes of their sounds tell them that some fish are nearby.

The killer whales catch the fish in their huge jaws. They swallow the fish whole or bite them into large pieces. When the baby whale is about three months old his teeth begin to grow. Now he can eat fish, too.

Every day the baby whale becomes a better swimmer. He learns to turn, twist, dive, and stand up straight on his tail. He pokes his head out of the water and sees some sea lions swimming near the shore.

sea lions

Sometimes killer whales hunt sea lions for food. The sea lions are safe today. The killer whales just filled up on fish. They are no longer hungry.

When a whale turns upright with its head out of the water, it is called spyhopping.

The baby killer whale is now one year old. He is twice as big as when he was born. He likes to play with the other young killer whales in the pod. They chase, push, and splash each other.

When the baby whale gets tired, he closes his eyes and floats. He may rest for a few minutes or a few hours. Then he is ready to play again.

When a whale goes underwater, its blowhole closes so water does not get in.

The young killer whale is now two years old. He can squeak, grunt, click, and whistle like the other whales in the pod. He listens for the sounds of whales as he swims.

As the young killer whale grows, his muscles get stronger. He gives himself a mighty push with his tail. His whole body bursts out of the water in a giant leap. He falls back with a huge splash.

When a whale leaps all the way out of the water, it is called breaching.

The young killer whale will stay with his family pod for his whole life. He will learn how to hunt with the other whales. He will get to know all the whales in his pod.

The young whale will reach his full size when he is about 20 years old. By then there will be new baby killer whales in the pod. They will join him and the other whales as they roam the ocean together in their daily search for food.

Where do killer whales live?

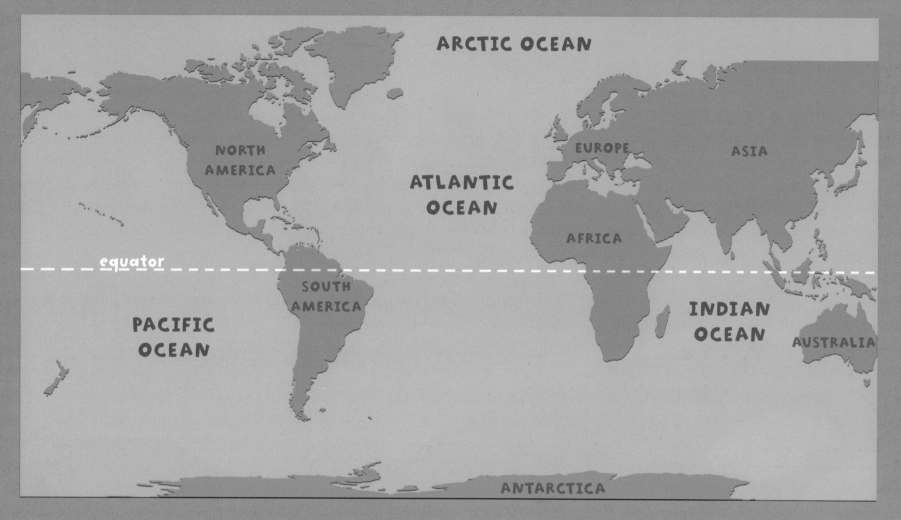

Killer whales are found in oceans all over the world, from icy waters near the poles to regions near the equator. They are most common in the Arctic, Antarctic, and places where the water is cold. Wild killer whales can often be spotted in the ocean off the west coasts of Canada and the United States. You can see killer whales in many marine parks and public aquariums.

KILLER WHALE FUN FACTS

Fast Swimmers

Killer whales are among the fastest animals in the ocean. They can swim at speeds of up to 30 miles (48 km) per hour.

Black and White

The markings of each killer whale are different. They may help the whales recognize one another. The gray patch behind the fin on the whale's back is called the saddle.

Tall Fins

The tall fin on a killer whale's back is its dorsal fin. It may be up to 6 feet (1.8 m) high! Males have tall, straight dorsal fins. Females have shorter fins that curve back.

A Killer Whale's Life

Some killer whales have lived as long as 80 years.

Listening to Echoes

Killer whales find their way around the ocean by making high pitched sounds and listening for echoes as the sounds bounce off objects around them. This method of navigating is called echolocation.

Staying Underwater

Killer whales need to breathe air, just like mammals that live on land. A killer whale may stay underwater for as long as 15 minutes. Usually, though, it comes up to breathe every four to five minutes.

Glossary

blowhole—*a hole on the top of a whale's head that is used for breathing*

blubber—*a thick layer of fat*

breaching—*when a whale leaps out of the water and then falls back in*

dorsal fin—*the tall fin on a whale's back*

echolocation—*listening for echoes and using them for direction and to find food*

equator—*an imaginary line around the middle of Earth; it divides the northern half from the southern half*

habitat—*the place and natural conditions in which a plant or an animal lives*

mammals—*warm-blooded animals who feed their babies milk*

nuzzle—*to touch or rub with the nose*

pod—*a family group of whales who live together*

saddle—*the gray patch behind the killer whale's dorsal fin*

spout—*a mist formed when a whale breathes out*

spyhopping—*when a whale turns upright with its head out of the water*

To Learn More

At the Library

Inskipp, Carol. *Killer Whale.* Chicago: Heinemann, 2005.

Le Bloas, Renée, and Jérôme Julienne. *The Orca, Admiral of the Sea.* Watertown, MA: Charlesbridge, 2001.

Markle, Sandra. *Killer Whales.* Minneapolis: Carolrhoda Books, 2004.

On the Web

FactHound offers a safe, fun way to find Internet sites related to this book. All of the sites on FactHound have been researched by our staff.

1. Visit *www.facthound.com*

2. Type in this special code for age-appropriate sites: 1404813217

3. Click on the FETCH IT button.

Your trusty FactHound will fetch the best sites for you!

Index

Look for all of the books in the Caroline Arnold's Animals series:

A Killer Whale's World   1-4048-1321-7
A Panda's World   1-4048-1322-5
A Penguin's World   1-4048-1323-3
A Zebra's World   1-4048-1324-1